EAU DE LEONE

(OH-DAY-LEE-OWN)

Water of the Lion
The Fountain of Youth

A collection of stories and Essays

BY JERRY METHNER

The Pathway to Wholeness

Hardcover: 978-1-953731-05-0
Paperback: 978-1-951505-68-4
eBook: 978-1-951505-67-7
Library of Congress Control Number: 2020916106

This is a work of nonfiction.

Ordering Information:

BookTrail Agency
8838 Sleepy Hollow Rd.
Kansas City, MO 64114

Printed in the United States of America

Have you had enough of pandemic?
Are you weary of "fake news"? Sick
and Tired of being sick and tired?
Want to loose weight, have a better job?
Have more friends (or maybe less)?

Whatever your desires, be aware of the
common factor in each scenario. YOU!!! You
are the key to bringing changes in your life.
Between the covers of Eau de Leone
are pearls of great value. Go diving and
see how many gems you can find.
You, who finds the most has the greatest reward!!!

Best Regards,

Jerry

BOOK SEGMENTS

- Endorsements
- Credits
- Philosophy
- The Kinslow System
- Why the Title "Eau de Leon"
- About Me
- My Family
- My Dad
- About Mom
- Intranspiration- Creating change
- Inspiration Your Ultimate Calling
- Creating Wellness
- Mind-Body Connection
- Giving Thanks
- Repetition
- American Institute of Stress
- Final Words
- The Best for Last

INTRODUCTION

Have you had enough of pandemics? Are you weary of so much "fake news"? Sick and tired of being sick and tired? Wish you could drop 15 or 20 pounds? Want to have a better job or an increase in your source of income? Wouldn't it be nice to have more friends or maybe less friends? Whatever you want to do, wherever you want to go, what ever your desire might be, just be aware of the one common element in each scenario. That one ingredient is YOU!

Ideally, someone other than yourself could make a quick fix for you. However, fortunately, you can have influence upon that person. For it is you.

Those who have eyes to see, ears to hear and minds willing to consider change will get the most from this book. A small percentage won't benefit from reading "Eau de Leone". Either its a waste of time or they could write a similar book of their own.

I had a good friend read through the rough draft looking for errors and suggestions to be made. She pointed out needs for punctuation, spelling and wording. But the greater suggestion was to explain more in depth the sources of many of my entries. To do that, I felt I'd need 2,000 pages or more. I prefer 200 pages or less. That number is about the quantity that I personally can absorb in a sitting. I want the nonreader or busy person not to be overwhelmed while getting a glimpse of where the book is heading.

Therefore, I might say "My thoughts come from the void," as suggested by Dr. Frank Kinslow from his book, "Quantum Living". Dr Kinslow states, "when our mind stops thinking so hard, the body relaxes and becomes rested and free from worry." Thus, thoughts are purer and God-like.

I would say that there is much information between the lines and written words on each page of this book. Even between each story or essay. Only when unbiased, rested or inspired can the reader or observer discern a more extensive awareness of the source from which inspiration appears.

EAU DE LEONE

(oh-day-lee-own)

Water of the Lion

The Fountain of Youth

A collection of stories and Essays
By Jerry Methner

The Pathway to Wholeness

INTENTIONALLY
LIVING EACH DAY
IN THE PRESENT

E vidence that there is a past can be found in remnants of existing ruins. Copies of ancient written accounts also testify of the past. Details of the past are formulated by examining those artifacts and projecting, via the mind and new technologies, what is the most likely probability of accuracy.

The future, however, is unknown in the present moment. At one time, space travel was but in the minds of dreamers who projected what might be. That was "unseen evidence" without yet time nor space attachment. Imaginations, in the minds of those that dreamed, became intentions in a vast field of possibilities.

Martin Luther King was one of many who had a dream which eventually became reality in the yet unseen realm of his present moment.

Super Jets and powerful rockets were but a hoped for thought in the minds of Wilbur and Orville Wright. Freedom and equality for all was an unseen hope in the mind of perhaps the most well-known president in US history, Abraham Lincoln. Who knows what was in the mind of George Washington? Certainly, more than cherry trees or one day having his picture on the dollar bill.

EAU DE LEONE
ENDORSEMENTS

I really don't have a long list of endorsers, which is not typical for most successful authors. Nope, this is what you get! Me! As a matter of fact, I haven't even read many books.

What? You say! Someone with 31 years of public-school teaching experience and a master's degree in educational administration.

One might say I was a stealth student. Got my high school book reports from the inside jackets of books. I don't even recall ever borrowing someone else's old report. But we might be surprised to find out how often that has happened. "Stealth students" resort to clever means to accomplish required levels of achievement. Or, many others simply drop out of school and get a job at a local place of employment. That isn't necessarily bad. Being happy in what you are doing is most important.

Others are much more stealthy and create ways to drain off the fat of this prosperous and great nation of ours.

Now if I could locate him, I know of someone who might endorse my book. That would be a quiet little sixth grade boy whom I tutored. He was a member of the local Chippewa Tribe of Native Americans. Three others in the class accompanied him. We'll call him Tommy for privacy purposes.

The four of them came to me regularly for assistance in strengthening reading skills. Now, I knew much about people lacking reading skills. As one of Robin Williams' humorous lines in his movie "Mrs. Doubtfire," stated, "I used to be one of them!" So, I knew what these boys were up against.

Each day at the conclusion of the lesson, I would use a little skittles candy activity. In turn, each boy would receive a reward of one tiny skittle, just for being there. Additionally, they would get a chance to earn a second skittle.   I would, secretly, randomly select another skittle, hiding it in the cup of my hand. I would then show the other three boys. We would concentrate on the color of the skittle to 'help' the guesser name the correct color. If they guessed it correctly, they got to have and eat that candy.

With today's virus fears I might have been socially reprimanded for risking the possibility of spreading Coronavirus in handing out candies.

The odds of guessing the right color correctly were one in five, or 20%. (Better than the odds of winning a game on Bingo Night.) Tommy, bless his heart, would never miss on his first 'guess' each time. Then, he would smile a proud sheepish grin. Now, what are the odds of that happening? Probably the same as winning the lotto.

Before long, the others increased their probability of choosing accurately. Maybe 40% or better. When Tommy turns of age, perhaps I'll take him to buy me a lotto ticket. LOL

I also am grateful to these authors and their books from which I've gleaned information and insight with which to define and guide my life strategies. Their research and writings have provided that which I need to state facts to which I ascribe in this book.

"The Holy Bible" Author: God

"Virus of the Mind" Author: Richard Brodie

"You've Already got it" Author: Andrew Wommack, Evangelist

"You are the Placebo" Author: Dr Joe Dispenza

"The Secret of Quantum Living" Author: Dr. Frank Kinslow

"Change your Thoughts-Change Your Life" Author: Dr Wayne Dyer

"Biology of Belief" Author: Bruce H Lipton, PhD

"Emergence: Seven Steps to radical life change" Author: Derek Rydall, American Screenwriter

CREDITS

There are countless nameless people who have impacted my life greatly. Most were encouragers who allowed me the freedom and motivation to experience abundant life. A few even endured considerable pain and disappointment as a consequence of choices I selfishly made. I am rather sorrowful about that.

But I will name the two for which I am eternally grateful. That is my dad and mom, Leon and Helen Methner. For their sacrifices on my behalf I believe they rest in peace.

PHILOSOPHY

My philosophy is very simple and clear: "All of creation is innately Good!" That's it. But, you might ask, "How can that be with so many seeming injustices. What about the cruelty, pain and warfare. while it is recorded in the Book of Genesis on the Bible, each day of the creation, God says, "And it is good."

Well, it is still potentially good, but people have, from the beginning, had disagreements. Perhaps minor initially. Maybe Eve told Adam, "Please put another leaf on your backside." Adam might have said something like, "You know I like bananas. Why do you insist on me eating applesauce?"

As the earth's population continued to grow, more personalities showed up. Little disagreements kept getting bigger as arguments occurred. Eventually, someone would get really hurt. I suspect that God had to finally say something like, "Enough! You're out of here."

Divisions continued to grow until God had to get rid of most of the population. They initially naively thought the abundant rainfall would be good for their crops. A conversation at that point could have been, "It's getting kind of deep." "I think we'd better get out of this thunderstorm. Seems like it's been doing this for days and days, about 40 Maude."

"Maude, did you close the windows?" "Maude, maybe we should go next door and see that foolish guy with the big ridiculous floating bathtub." "Maude... Maude...gurgle...gurgle... Here we go again! When will we ever learn?"

Initially, creation was intended to be all GOOD but that can't happen until all of mankind changes their thinking about relationships. You heard me right, I said ALL! Not just the guys on the other team, nation or color. We tend to have a need to blame someone and it's never me!

I believe that's what Wayne Dyer was getting at when he wrote his book "Change Your Thoughts-Change Your Life." Until that happens, history will just continue to repeat over and over. Wouldn't it be nice if everyone were just like sweet to me?

Even within cultures and or religions, one group will say to another, basically, "My way or the highway."

All Is Good despite how things appear to the human eye. All of creation is ultimately good if we look at it with the eyes of our hearts.

Shall we banish all control freaks? Needing to be in control reminds me of a humorous analogy that states: "The need to be in control is like having a fraternity party in a Monastery, and just as welcome!"

The following is from a blog by Dr Frank Kinslow. I recorded it 2/1/2014. It is in reference to his healing system which he teaches worldwide.

THE RULE OF TWO

1. The Principle of Universal Harmony dictates there is always order in the universe even when there appears to be none.

2. The world is not as I see it. It is impossible for me to know, feel or perceive everything for any given situation and therefore my comprehension must be incomplete. Life is

basically JOYFUL. If I'm not feeling that, my perception is not reflecting that reality. Our lives need to be free flowing. Holding onto people, ideas and things disrupts the flow. We are all the same yet completely different. We bond through our sameness. Our differences add sweetness to our sameness. When these two opposites find balance, all things benefit.

EAU DE LEONE

(water of the lion)

Juan Ponce de Leon "Fountain of Youth"

WHY THE TITLE, "EAU DE LEONE?"

I nitially I wanted to encourage friends or even strangers to create life conditions of health and satisfying experiences. Since then, I've decided that it's not my direct responsibility. Rather, just be kind and encouraging. It's not for me to tell another how to do this unless specifically asked for my advice.

Back now to my title, "Eau de Leone." I remember in my high school history experience, hearing of an explorer from Spain. His name was Juan Ponce de Leone. He was credited with exploring what is now named Florida.

Supposedly, he was in search of "The Fountain of Youth." After doing some research, my conclusion was that his Florida explorations only lasted a short time. More of his searching was in Puerto Rico. Where he eventually served two terms as the Puerto Rican Governor.

Intrigued by the thought of the myth surrounding "The Fountain of Youth", I once gave a lecture about the concept of having a natural spring in which one could bathe regularly to experience increased health and beauty benefits. The final conclusion that I emphasized was that the real "Fountain of Youth" exists only within us. It is enhanced by proper diet, exercise and rest. That must be accompanied by a firm intention to stick to it no matter what the mirror and weight scale try to contradict, more or less what our natural senses try to convince us.

After all, every other media ad tells you of all the pills, lotions and operations to make you feel and look younger and healthier. (The side effects are usually left out.) Actually, by means of applying the "Placebo Effect" one can make themselves feel younger and healthier. But, once you quit believing it, you continue aging and experiencing ailments. I say, that's what you mistakenly believe.

I hopefully desire to help others experience a healthier, happier life journey. Unless you exercise faith, only the size of a mustard seed, you're on the "good luck plan." By the way, that faith thing cannot be accompanied by any measure of unbelief.

I'll hope to be describing some of the beginner's methods of making desired changes. I plan face to face dialogues with you and others. That is one of my personal intentions. In my imaginations I'm already doing that so as long as I apply my own words, it's as good as already done.

(insert text secrets) So many people in the world are kind and giving yet struggle with finances health and relationships

Now I'd like to share some of my own personal history. In doing so, I hope you'll better understand where I'm coming from.

ABOUT ME

I was born in a small rented house in Beaverton, Michigan on September 5, 1939. At age 4 my family moved to a small farm just outside of town. The farm was owned by my grandfather, Frank Methner. That's where my middle name came from, Jerry Frank Methner. My grandparents had lived on the family farm for many years. Eventually Grandpa Frank had a serious stroke and could neither talk plainly nor walk more than one unsteady shuffle at a time.

I remember, when my older siblings would irritate grandpa, then retreat to the safety of the upstairs steps. They'd watch as grandpa would shuffle along shaking his finger (the pointer) at each of us. (Except sweet Jerry.) His muttering sounded kind of like kunny-kunny-kay.

As kids we hadn't yet developed the character trait of compassion. We were just adventuresome "characters" at best. Besides, it was kind of exciting. Sort of like getting away from a fearful ogre. We didn't fully understand about strokes, nor why grandpa acted that way. After grandpa passed on, I suspect that he forgave us. I attended Beaverton schools through high school. Upon graduation, I went to Lamoni, Iowa where I earned a BA in Elementary Education at Graceland College.

In 1962, I got my first teaching job. I taught 6th grade science at Flat Rock, Michigan. A year later, I moved to Midland, Michigan. There I was a 4th grade classroom teacher and Head Teacher in a four-room school building for the

Bullock Creek School System. During the three summers in Midland I earned my MA degree at Central Michigan University, majoring in Elementary School Administration.

Two years later I moved to Rudyard in Michigan's Upper Peninsula. There I would spend the next 28 years at a variety of assignments. This included being Building Principal of an elementary school with an enrollment of over 500 K-6 children and more than 30 staff members. My final three years of teaching I was gifted by working with small groups of special children in need of help developing reading skills. What a way to end my career!

When my teaching career ended, a new career began. I would spend the next 26 years learning and building the A-One Chimney Service. That gave me much satisfaction serving thousands of customers across the Eastern end of the

Upper Peninsula of Michigan. I still have many customers that I have annually served even to the present time. A-Chimney has become so well respected and requested that advertising isn't even a major priority. Word of mouth and customer recommendations keep us busy. Even potential competitors cooperate by sending us customers.

Growing up on the farm afforded me many opportunities to learn about animals, birds and bees, and machinery. Depending on the good Lord, I learned about successfully growing crops.

We had a little of everything. Cattle, pigs, rabbits and chickens. Cats and dogs, pigeons and sparrows and lots of room to run. The shoes came off when summer vacation began. They stayed off most of the time except for Sunday mornings to go to church.

My feet were tough enough to run full speed down the gravel road without flinching. Then we could step over into a patch of poison ivy with never any consequences. The crowning glory was to accidentally step into a fresh pile of cow poop. That stuff would squeeze up between the toes-yucky!

To a large extent we were somewhat like a Ma and Pa Kettle type family. Sunday eves the four of us kids would sit lined up beside each other on the sofa next to the radio, no Tv's. We'd listen to our favorite mystery programs; "The Shadow," "Charlie Chan," "Sam Spade" and a few others.

One year we raised four little piglets in the far corner of the kitchen. I think something had happened to the oldest sow. We each claimed and named one. Sally, Stu, Satin and Suzy. I think Satan was my older brother's. Who ever heard of such a thing? To this day my siblings and I recall and laugh about that experience.

Speaking of raising pigs, one of my most memorable experiences had to do with some of our pigs. We were sort of poor, some of our fences had holes in them. One day the two old sows and their litters of baby pigs found one of those holes and squeezed under it. Dad and I soon set out to find them. When we did, getting them back through the hole was a different set of circumstances.

Now dad was quite a taskmaster on the farm. Sort of the Alpha Male type personality when it came to letting the animals know who was boss. He made it very clear. He had no fear.

Dad began chasing those pigs, past the hole several times. Stick in hand, he began hollering with the pigs snorting and howling like angry lions. I found it too frightening and retreated to a nearby tree. There, I sort of began to pray.

Eventually dad forced the pigs back through the fence. Once done, we walked behind the pigs back to the barn. I think I said something like, "We got that done didn't we Dad." (After all, I did pray.)

A few weeks later, the pigs got out again. This time it was my job to find them all by myself. As I searched, in the back of my mind I recalled the frightening roars of the old sows as dad had chased them back and forth before finally getting them through the hole in the fence. Terrifying to a ten-year-old boy. Me!

When I found the pigs, they were on the other side of a really good fence. Our neighbor had lots more money than we had. I began to coax the pigs along the fence row looking for a hole. "Shoo piggy piggy." We walked the entire width of the field, but no holes.

At the edge of the field we came to a deep ditch, at the bottom of which was a wet wallow. The pigs began enjoying it very much on that hot summer day. Just great! Now what do I do? In my mind I could still recall the terrible, lion-like roar of the old sow a week earlier when Dad had tried to force her through the fence.

This time, I prayed a real prayer. Even got down on my knees. I no sooner got my amen said than the lead female pig got up out of the muddy wallow and squeezed through a small hole in the fence. It seemed only about half the size of her body. The remainder of the pig family followed making only a contended grunt, oink-oink sound. Think I'll use that technique of praying again. As I followed the pig herd, perhaps I was thinking "we got 'er done again didn't we Daddy God!"

Having given credit specifically to my parents, I'd like to share a few details about who they really were to the best of my recollection.

DAD

My dad was like a third or fourth generation Christian. His dad, my grandpa Frank, was one of eighteen children. Can't even imagine what life was like for them.

My dad worked hard to become a public-school teacher. Many of those years he taught vocal and instrumental music. This had a significant influence on my appreciation of music. I'll always recall how proud my maternal grandmother was when I was awarded the Arion Award for music leadership at my senior class awards night. To this day, I actively participate, at age 80, with my church worship band every Sunday. It is called a worship team, not a choir.

Dad was an extremely kind and empathetic person. He took pride, as high school band director, in the performances both in concerts and in marching parades. He would also conduct the band in formations at Friday night football games during half time. As a baritone player, I always took part.

After more than 20 years as band director and vocal music instructor, he moved to Garden City, Michigan. For the first time, dad became a 5th grade classroom teacher. He continued at that position until retirement.

I recall at that time the teachers' organization had a surprise retirement dinner for him. Over 200 teachers and staff were present to honor dad. What a rewarding event for a thirty plus year veteran educator.

Dad enjoyed retirement. He and mom traveled quite a bit and spent winters in Florida and Arizona.

Dad passed away peacefully at my nephews in Florida in 1986. Mom said on the night of his passing that she went into the bedroom to check on him. He laid sleeping in bed with arms waving in the air directing his band. What a way to pass on to the next phase of his journey.

I had a taped recording of him singing the Lord's Prayer from a previous occasion. We played it at his funeral. My siblings and I kidded about that. Yep, that's dad. Wouldn't miss his own funeral.

I never have difficulty remembering the years of his birth and death. Halley's Comet came by in 1910, the year of his birth. It reappeared again in 1986, the year he died. Or, did he really die? I'll leave that up to you. I shared that with one of my school classmates and he said, "Wow, that made the hair stand up on my arms."

I do not have quite the notable way to remember my mom's birth and death years. I only recall that she was four years younger than dad.

ABOUT MOM

Mom's life history was somewhat different than Dad's. I do now that I felt loved and favored by her among my older two siblings.

Mom was the second of five girls in her family. Her oldest sister spent quite a few years in and out of mental institutional care. Actually, mom and the other three sisters had some problems dealing with who they were. They were high strung, in my opinion, and even had mentally related conditions, whatever that means. That had nothing to do with their intelligence. I think that they were all either valedictorian, salutatorian or ranked high in their high school class standings.

When I grew into adulthood, my ex-spouse shared with me accounts of incidents which mom had told her. Apparently, her dad, my maternal grandfather, had been a womanizer. Mother told of a time when grandpa took her with him on one of his flings. Mom said she purposely wet her pants while sitting on the lady's lap.

Another confidence mom shared was that she had an abortion after my older brother was born. This would have been about a year before I came along.

Who knows why that happened? It was certainly a time of local unrest. The fears attached to WWII were rampant. Shortages and the loss of lives of young men and women in the war made life stressful. Who would want to bring a child into uncertainties such as those?

I'll forever be grateful that mother didn't repeat the abortion decision with the next pregnancy. That was me! I am truly blessed.

Perhaps that was related to the reason that I've always felt favored. My parents always encouraged me while yet allowing me to make my own choices. Here's an ode I wrote about my mom.

"Praises to mom,
took the cards she was dealt
And held them close to her heart.
Played her only ace to light up my face
From her love I never will part."

Perhaps her aborted embryo was me, but I was too determined to not give in to that fact. "Give me a second chance 'cuz I have a mission in life."

I vaguely recall, as a very young child, having dream-like impressions that almost seemed real. They might best be described as watching, up close, a bowling ball approaching me, about to crash into an intended target right in front of me. Most noticeably, was the unstoppable rotation of the ball. Funny thing was that it always stopped short just before it could strike anything.

I'm no psychologist but wonder if that was somehow strangely related to the time period before and following my actual birth. I was somehow aware in the womb of the trauma mom was going through. Certainly not on a conscious level. Mere curiosity now.

My mother more than compensated by her kindness to me, for the decision not to repeat an abortion. All my life I've felt that I was special to her. It was something that I believe she might have struggled with much of her life.

I feel that perhaps my mother compensated with favoritism toward me for even the memory of having to choose abort or don't abort!

Intranspiration,
Process of creating Change

Intranspiration is a new word that I made up. You won't find it in a dictionary.....Yet! However, it does have great significance. There are three primary elements to the Intranspiration process. Segments of the new word can be found in each of the three steps. In-trans-pi-ration.

The focus is to develop a personal plan that leads to basic happiness as defined in degrees of health, relationships and wealth. I'm not defining wealth as merely a means of getting money. Too much of that already exists.

It has been suggested time and again, that it just doesn't get 'er done! Theoretically, it is believed by some that if all the monetary wealth in the world was divided evenly to everyone, in a few short years it would be proportionately back in the hands of individuals at approximately the same levels. The conclusion: Through your intentions either concentrate on creating more income (you might regret it); being contented with the way things currently are; or down size (you'll be okay).

Primary credit for the steps I'm about to outline I give to authors Dispenza, Lipton and Wommack. Information contributed by the other named authors is interwoven with my own personal perspectives.

Actually, if I was making it a contest, but I'm not, the hands down leader would have to be the author with the most copies sold, longest running tenure and impact on the largest number of people. Hands down, no contest, must be God and his book "The Holy Bible."

If I could influence even less than one percent of his numbers, I would be the happiest person in the world and for all of time. It's not about religion but rather relationships.

I've read or heard from several sources that state imagination as being one of the most powerful human forces in all of the universe. It has inspired many people throughout the history of civilization, to achieve great objectives.

You and many others have created a sort of a bucket list of things you wish would show up or take place in your life. Let me tell ya darlin', it ain't likely to occur. A wish, in and of itself, is like firing a blank cartridge at a target.

It's essential to choose a clearly stated intention that is relatively easy to attain, for your first time. Success with this one will plant the seed of confidence in the fertile soil of your mind for future successes. That increases the likelihood that future intentions will likewise follow successfully.

An intention for example might be, "I have that fashionable new pair of boots that are so in." That's a pretty clearly stated intention. Also, it's important to make it as though you already have it. Otherwise it's just the same as a wish firing blanks.

Let's start intranspirationing. LOL

The first element of INTRANSPIRATION has to do with INFORMATION. You, the seeker, will benefit from gathering as much related information as is necessary to support your original intention. Clearly state that intention repeatedly.

You can actually become a new personality. Hold onto that image until it eventually becomes real. Don't give up or stop lest you risk disconnection.

The second element is Transformation. In the Bible in Romans 12:2 it says "Don't be conformed to the world's way of thinking and acting. Rather be transformed by the renewing of your mind." Transformed mind leads to that new personality. New perspective!

Now comes the beginning of the pay off. You're about to unearth the mother lode. The mining process is about to begin. Shift into gear (or simply put it into automatic forward.)

The information and transformation steps have laid the foundation for the third element. INSPIRATION.

INSPIRATION YOUR ULTIMATE CALLING

"What is necessary to change a person is to change his awareness of himself." (A Maslow) It is shifting the belief system that you might have that says, "I don't have the talent. I am limited. I can't...Things never...etc."

INSPIRATION is when an idea gets hold of you and takes you where you were supposed to go originally. We must be like The Source from which we came. We are a piece of God, a divine source. Our essence is our greatness. We must be what we came from. When you move into spirit, you leave behind the false self. You have the capacity of knowing that you can do anything. The false self is simply ego. (limitations & impossibility) Edging God Out! Ego says who we are is:

1.)   What we have

2.)   What we do

3.)   What others think I am

According to Patanjali, an ancient philosopher, when you are inspired by some great purpose, some extraordinary project, six things happen:

1.)   All your thoughts break their bonds! Bonds are thoughts that keep you disconnected from your source (out of harmony with spirit). You attract what it is you're thinking. What I desire, that is aligned with Spirit, is on it's way. I desire it! There's nothing to fuss about! Nikos Kazentazakis, author of "Zorba The Greek," stated that: "By believing passionately in that which does not exist, we create it. That which is nonexistent has not been sufficiently desired."

2.) Your mind transcends limitations! Transcending limitations means entering into the field of all possibilities. (nothing left out) You become unlimited in the exact same way as before you showed up on earth. There is nothing more powerful than an idea whose time has come. When you stay connected to it, it can't be stopped.

3.) Your consciousness expands in every direction!

Expanding consciousness means finding oneself doing things that you don't understand why you're doing them. (When you have a feeling that this is something you have to do). You can't be stopped from doing it.

4.) You find yourself in a new, great and wonderful world!

The whole world changes and you listen to that feeling. "Every tree in the meadow seems to be dancing. Those with average eyes will see as fixed and still." When being touched deeply by living inspired (in spirit), the world in which you lived no longer exists. Things not noticed before begin coming alive.

5.) Dormant forces, faculties and talents come alive!

Dormant forces are forces you thought were inaccessible, not available, synchronicities, serendipity. You are having a thought and because of that, it manifests. You act as God acts, constantly giving and forgiving. True nobility is not about being better than anyone else. It's about being better than you used to be. When in spirit, we move away from feeling sorry for self, but rather look for the lessons to be learned.

6.) You discover yourself to be a greater person by far than you ever dreamed yourself to be.

You become a greater person by practicing radical humility. The only way to convert an enemy to a friend is through love. There is no other way. You live and breathe love in every way. An essential principle for living an inspired life is to remember that our desires don't arrive on our schedule. They arrive when they're supposed to.

Neural networks are firing and wiring in your brain. Literally, new circuits are forming. Your body is getting it's orders and is prepared to "git 'er done." You enter a state of elevated emotion. You're excited as you continue to fuel those feelings. Don't feel that excited? Fake it until you finally do. Your body doesn't know the difference and is not in the business of judging whether good or bad. (Jerry, I thought you said in your philosophy that all is innately good. Oops!)

An absolute essential at this point is to Give Thanks! "What," you say, "when I'm feeling so excited?" Give thanks in all things, at all times. Stop thinking or your engines of creating begin to slow and are in danger of stalling completely.

Start to feel disappointed? Give Thanks!

Somebody messing with you? Give Thanks!

Running out of money and resources? Give Thanks!

Do you get the point or do I need to give you ten more examples? GIVE THANKS!!! Give thanks IN all things. Don't give thanks FOR all things, but in whatever the conditions.

To allow any degree of unbelief can be the death of your original intentions. SO, keep the faith baby!

The Bible states clearly that "faith is the assurance of things hoped for and the substance of things not seen." Hebrews 11:1. Hope is translated as 'earnest expectations.' "Things not seen,' only refers to what you can't see with your physical sight. You've got to see them in your imagination even before they show up in your physical vision. Try it! You'll like it.

I attended a retreat over thirty years ago, during which a married couple taught a class in reference to faith. Each day, they stated that our greatest sins are fear, doubt and unbelief because they distract from that which God labels as possible. And, did you know that the word 'sin' was also an archery term that simply meant to miss the target. So, if you're missing your target, your intention, just knock another arrow in the string of your bow. Don't pout and beat your head on the ground. Get up and knock another arrow in your bow. Pretty simple, huh? Nobody's going to punish you for being a bad boy or girl. You do enough self- punishment to yourself than all the critics ever could.

So, if you don't see your intention with your physical eyes, see it once and for all in your imagination. Don't give up! It will show up! Persist!

As a hobby, I enjoy making homemade wine. I mostly give it away or have a small sip before going to bed. The Bible says it's good for the belly! I learned from an old professional wine maker that a highly important ingredient in the process of making a good wine, is simply exercise patience. Bottle it too soon and you'll have an explosion. Allow foreign contaminating particles in and it goes sour. BE PATIENT!

As you seek to pursue whatever your clear intention is, stick with it to completion. Your inner self will let you know what to do if you don't rush it before it's time. Be patient!

In the past year, I have used the intranspiration process to overcome maladies in me that were uncomfortable in the least. After ten years or more of acid reflux syndrome, I no longer experience that. It's gone. I go to sleep each night like a contented baby. No more acid reflux. Intranspiration!

I've also had several skin cancer-like nodes or small open sores. No more! The last small open sore finally healed over. No more bumping causing bleeding. Intranspiration.

A year ago, my chewing molars on my upper right jaw were very sensitive to the point that it was too painful to chew on that side. Now for the past six months I'm able to chew on either side with no pain. Intranspiration.

Whatever the intention of your desire, start small and grow confidently into greater accomplishments. If you're still with me, let's continue.

CREATING WELLNESS

J aun Ponce de Leon, one of the early explorers to America, is credited for having sought a "Fountain of Youth." That mystic condition was intended to create features and likeness of being youthful simply by bathing in that pool. In doing so, one could supposedly experience qualities of feeling and living healthy. Or, at least, maintaining a lifestyle free of pain and suffering.

An act of doing so also included making wise selections of dieting to enhance a healthy body. Interestingly, I was watching a talk show a number of years ago that addressed that very topic. I wasn't paying particularly close attention to the conversation, when I heard the interviewer state "so, what I hear you saying is that what one THINKS about what they're eating is just as significant as the actual value of the food."

I've found that this is very much so. It's a good case for praying over food before eating, or at least giving thanks.

If Ponce de Leone had known about body science, he'd have wanted good genes in the water of his fountain. Of course, many know that the genes passed on by one's parents are of great significance determining a healthy state of being. It's also known that certain qualities are passed on in the inherited genes which are not necessarily helpful.

You may have heard statements made like, "oh, yes cancer genes have been passed on to every other generation of my family tree." By the way, stupidity and ignorance genes may be included in every generation of many family trees. Or it might have been said, "Gramps and Granny had naturally purple hair, so there's a likelihood that I might have purple hair too." "Yes, and make that curly as well."

It is true that inherited genes are passed on from generation to generation. However, believe it or not, those characteristic manifestations can be changed. That's right, I said they can be changed.

Enter Dr Bruce Lipton. Dr Lipton taught University level biology for many years. Gradually, he began to realize that what he had been teaching was not a fixed reality. After considerable testing in his lab, he now teaches that genes are not at all fixed but rather they are subject to being changed.

In his book, "Biology of Belief," Bruce goes into great detail presenting supportive facts of telling how this all works. If you're a details type of person, I highly recommend that you get Bruce's book personally. I'm actually a "Genetic Soup for the Soul" kind of guy.

Epigenetics (above the gene) discloses that genes and their influences can indeed be changed or modified. Bruce describes that every gene is but a blueprint of one's likelihood in determining genetic destiny, a destiny that can be altered. "How can that be?" You might wonder.

Granny's relatives always have had Humpty Dumpty Syndrome. That's why they're so prone to falling off walls all the time. All the King's horses and men couldn't seem to help them.

Then, along comes the Good Doctor Lipton with his cauldron of magic potion. I think it's called "Lipton's Tea Brew." He got all those with Humpty Dumpty syndrome back together again merely by having a sip of Lipton's Tea, or maybe it was Prince Charming and Rumplestilskin. Or was it Snow White and the Seven Bears? Goldilocks was a hot blonde chick because her Granny had curly blond hair.

Back to real life, Dr Bruce Lipton discovered that the blueprint that is called a gene can be taken back to the drawing board," for alterations work. To discover how this is done one must read Dr. Lipton's book, "Biology of Belief."

For the most part, it's important to learn how to change your thoughts. You might just wonder what is a thought? According to Dr. Frank Kinslow from his book, "Quantum Living," "thoughts are a form of mental energy, sparks of spirit, igniting the mind and everything they touch." Thought, according to Dr Kinslow, comes from the void, nothing, when our mind stops thinking so hard, the body relaxes and becomes rested free from worry.

Wow, that having been said, let's just chill and relax a lot more. Oops, almost forgot, we've got to work overtime and ignore the children so that we don't have to worry about making the big payment on the new car, like the one the Jones have. Then we can go to the cottage, sweep up the mouse turds, chase the mosquitoes, wash the windows, paint the trim and reset the critter traps.

After that we can rest! Oh no, it's time to go home to work and save enough money for next year's vacation.

I think I'll choose more of just do nothing and be happy. How can you have more of nothing? You figure it out.

I have so much more to disclose that I don't think this book will ever end being written. If I don't write it, other inspired writers will continue. Perhaps they will have a slightly different perspective. But if it isn't acted upon, with changes being made in the collective behaviors of the human race, pain, suffering and poverty will continue to exist.

A final bit of information I Will leave with you. Since change can be so difficult in many cases, let me point out a major hurdle that must be dealt with. That is the mind-body-relationship. It can't be ignored if any measurable degree of success is to be achieved. They must be on the same page at the same time. Total agreement is the only acceptable condition for mind and body. What makes it most difficult is that there are two parts of you (actually, more than that) with potentially separate agendas.

To make this union a bit on the light side, I offer this amusing poem.

Mind Body Connection

When Mr. Body met young Miss Mind
A finer couple you could not find
Now Mr. Body knew he was great
He'd learned it all by the age of eight
He could do anything with his eyes not open
That wasn't exactly what Miss Mind was hopin
She thought she'd give him a little nudge
But the stubborn Mr. Body wouldn't even budge
So, Miss Mind gave Mr. Body a piece of her mind
Now Mr. Body follows close behind
So, Body don't try to flex a muscle
Or you'll be on a leash with
your head in a muzzle.

In the true mind-body connection, old habits need to be broken in order to make desired changes. An elevated emotion is necessary to do so. Also, friends and acquaintances, or even strangers, may try to interfere. A persistent commitment to a desired intention is an absolute necessity. May you be strong and successful in your intentions!

Hope to see and hear you in person soon.

Jerry

GIVING THANKS

The action of giving thanks, when faithfully applied is like incorporating unseen factors. In fact, it is equally important to give thanks at the beginning of an intention as it is at the completion. Leaving out either one puts you on the front line wishing without a loaded weapon. Give thanks at the beginning and the end, the Alpha and the Omega.

It doesn't matter what language or in which culture it's given. Give thanks in all things and at all times. In doing so, that unseen helper factor is engaged.

Ephesians 6:12 "For we are not contending against physical things, but against ideologies and powers of this present timing."

You might be thinking, "when is this guy going to quit this giving thanks overkill". The answer is a very simple NEVER!!!

REPETITION

What's with this repetition stuff? Your worst enemy in completing the fulfillment of your intentional task isn't even an enemy at all. What? How can an enemy not be an enemy? Just doesn't make sense.

Your body operates under the influence of your subconscious mind. It was programmed to act according to it's "hard drive" which was installed mostly before the age of eight. Eventually it became so addicted to that program that your conscious mind goes right along with the body. Habits have formed. Talk about a difficult thing to change. I'd rather teach an old dog new tricks than to get you to change your thoughts.

"Change your thoughts, change your life." Only problem is, you can't do it simply by thinking you can. Your body has a mind of its own, so to speak. You and others have programmed it's learned agenda. Your body is nonjudgmental. It just does what it has been taught. That's the most difficult thing to change. It can most effectively be managed by repeatedly telling it over and over that the intention which you desire is already a reality. Body won't even know the difference.

I'm going to close now with this information from the American Institute of Stress. "The type A Behavior concept"

Napoleon's favorite physician, Corvisart, wrote that heart disease was due to "the passions of the mind, anger, madness, fear, jealousy, terror, love, despair, joy, avarice, stupidity and ambition.

Certainly, we have all experienced at least one or several of these "passions of the mind." To learn more about stress and its effect on your life and in your wellbeing, go to The American Institute of Stress online.

Now you have your homework. Get to it and be healthy!

With all sincerity,

Jerry

FINAL WORDS

(Until the next final words)

There will likely never be final words from me. It seems that each time I think my book is done, something unexpected appears. That is perhaps the best final word that I might give today. Be open to a new experience or a different perception of what you think you already know. Life will always be one awareness after another. Ultimately, do more of nothing and just be surprised by what shows up.

THE BEST FOR LAST

I must emphasize and honor the extreme dedication and commitment of the medical community and first responders. Many have made the ultimate sacrifice in service to our great nation.

My suggested methods of change and improvement are intended to be in cooperation, certainly not competition with the historical advances.

Some of my closest and trusted friendships include workers in the fields of mental health, psychological, chiropractic and physicians.

The thoughts, opinions and suggested actions reflected in my writing are not to be substitutes for professional and medical opinions and diagnosis.

May we all toil together to make the world, the entire universe to be the best that is possible. All things are possible.....

Author speaking to 400 people at business
success attunement seminar in

Agate ring crafted from stones
found by Lake Superior

Agate pendant from Lake Superior. 1 ounce gold Jerry panned from Crisso

Creator, Owner, Operator A1 Chimney
Service 26 years running

Ounce Ruby Jerry dug from Cowee
mountain Ruby mine

_Jerry's Collection of agates and semi
precious gemstones from Lake Supe...

Jerry Methner.

Jerry's collection of rings

CPSIA information can be obtained
at www.ICGtesting.com
Printed in the USA
LVHW012345111220
673999LV00007B/104